NEW YORK

Published in the United States by Del Rey, an imprint of Random House, a division of Penguin Random House LLC, New York.

Del Rey is a registered trademark and the Circle colophon is a trademark of Penguin Random House LLC.

Originally published in hardcover in the United Kingdom by Egmont UK Limited.

ISBN 978-0-593-15855-5
Ebook ISBN 978-0-593-15856-2

Printed in China on acid-free paper by RRD Asia Printing Solutions

Written by Thomas McBrien

Illustrations by Ryan Marsh

randomhousebooks.com

2 4 6 8 9 7 5 3 1

First US Edition

Design by John Stuckey, Jessica Coomber, Ian Pollard and Miranda Snow

MINECRAFT™
EPIC BASES

BUILDS TO SPARK YOUR IMAGINATION

CONTENTS

INTRODUCTION

Welcome to the HQ Realm! This realm is the home of the Twelve, a guild of expert builders who have dedicated their efforts to creating epic bases. For the first time ever, the Twelve have opened their gates and invited fellow adventurers to join them on a guided tour around their unique bases. Join us as we meet our hosts and hear all about their top tips and tricks.

ESCHER WONDER, GRAND ARCHITECT

A-hem. Welcome! As the leader of this guild, it is my pleasure to welcome you to Craftholme. This citadel is the face of modern architecture and a school for aspiring builders. Everything a builder could possibly need can be found here.

ALDUR BLUETOUCH, FROST KING

I'm the king of the cold! The brilliance of my ice and the strength of my walls are second to none, except perhaps to the might of my snow golems.

PROF. SHELLY SANDE, RESIDENT ARCHAEOLOGIST

Hi! I'm Shelly and I'm the team archaeologist. I'm captivated by the unsolved mysteries surrounding ancient structures, like who built all these temples? And why?

DR. ATTICUS SPARK, TRAVELING INVENTOR

Yes, yes, yes. It's me. The brilliant, magnificent, omnificent, world-renowned scientist, Dr. Atticus Spark. I'm an inventor at heart and my base is centered on scientific exploration.

GUNHILDA FENRIR, VIKING BERSERKER

Some call me brave. Others call me reckless. One thing is for certain: I'll wave my sword at anyone who dares get in my way. If you're ever in need of me, you can find me on my trusty longship, *Fenrir's Tooth*.

MARIA TRENCH, DEEP-SEA EXPLORER

My family, once powerful, lived in a grand underwater palace. It fell to ruin long ago, but I have restored it to its former glory, reinventing it as an underwater base.

KAT SEEKER, WILDERNESS EXPLORER
You've arrived! Great! I can't wait to show you what I've discovered in the jungle. My base is a field site for observation and research. Come on now, there's a lot to look at.

MISS LOLLY DELIGHT, CANDY QUEEN
Howdy! I'm Lolly Delight and I'm so happy you're here. I've been working hard to prepare my base with all the sweetest treats for the sweetest people. There's nothing I can't make with my super-special, super-secret building ingredient … *pssst*, it's sugar.

STEVEN STARGAZER, XENOARCHAEOLOGIST
Listen up! I'm Steven – builder, dreamer and alien expert. My building techniques are out of this world! I'm here to show you the latest in alien design and why it is undoubtedly the superior building style.

RITA THE REANIMATOR, HARBINGER OF DOOM
Hurry now! I must return home before dark. My base is the Macabre Motel, a delightfully spooky scare house. You won't be my only guests – just the only "living" ones.

SIR CORNELIUS LUCKLESS, PARANOID KNIGHT
Thy luck has proven true, for thou hast seekest and found the greatest knight in all the realms. Dark mysteries and hidden dangers lurk around every corner, but I have built a mighty fortress to keep evil at bay. Let us stay vigilant. One can never be too careful.

FLINT SCREE, FORGE LORD
Uh … My passion is … uh … minerals. And ores. Yes, I really like ores. Shiny gold ingots, glistening emeralds, unbreakable diamonds. Just wait until you see my treasure trove!

GENERAL BUILD TIPS

You too could be an expert builder. It's easier than you could possibly imagine! I know firsthand that building large-scale bases can be difficult at first, so I've asked my fellow expert builders to share some of their top tips so that you too can create an epic base. You'll see just what you can create when you follow these tips and marvel at our bases.

PLANNING 1

CREATIVE MODE
In Creative mode, you'll be able to build a base incredibly quickly and easily with unlimited access to all the blocks in the game and the freedom of movement that all adventurers envy. If you're looking for a real challenge, you can build your base in Survival mode, but make sure you're well stocked with the necessary blocks!

PLANNING
Good planning is at the heart of all epic builds. Without proper preparation, even the most modest of creations can go awry. Step one is to decide what you want to build: a castle, a school, a spaceship – it can be anything you like. Think about what you need from your base and tailor your design appropriately.

THEME
Once you've planned what you want to build, it's time to pick a theme that works with your ideas. Browse through the available blocks for inspiration and pick out your favorite ones. Consider how you can use them together and what sort of aesthetic you are looking for. Be creative!

STRUCTURE

Getting the structure of your construction right is crucial to ensure that everything goes to plan. Our builders recommend setting some basic structure outlines with marker blocks before you begin. Pick a bright, easy-to-spot block as a marker so you can locate it easily. The Twelve like to use lime concrete!

TERRAFORMING

Once you know what to build, you need to decide where to build it. Pick an ideal biome for your theme and don't hesitate to alter the land to your liking.

BLOCK CHOICE

Time to get building! Select the key building blocks for your base. These will be some of the most important blocks on your base, so make sure you think carefully about what you want. It will save time and avoid frustration if you make the decisions before starting construction.

DECORATIONS

Make sure your visitors have no doubts whose home they are visiting! Add a few personal touches to make the base unique to you. Are you an adventurer? Put some of your treasures into item frames. Are you a mob collector? Build displays for each of your favorite mobs. Perhaps you're an inventor? Create a museum for all of your best creations.

FINISHING DETAILS

Finishing details are the difference between a good base and an epic one. Consider adding plants, tinted windows and other decorations to make your creations stand out. Don't forget about the surrounding area! Small touches can go a long way. Pathways, streetlamps and outbuildings are fantastic finishing details to consider.

ANCIENT MUMMY'S TOMB

Many years ago, I stumbled across a secret entrance hidden in the side of a sand dune, which led me to an ancient underground desert temple. This discovery presented me with the perfect opportunity to build a tomb in the style of the ancient architects. It had to be impressive, imposing and fit for a pharaoh — I knew just what to build. Welcome to my desert tomb!

DESERT VILLAGE

DESERT OASIS
Tall trees, colorful plants and pooling water are all signs of a rich, vibrant ecosystem.

PROFESSOR SHELLY SANDE
Resident Archaeologist

WATER BEARER STATUES

FIRE BEARER STATUES

GRAND ENTRANCE

RIVERS FLANKED BY PILLARS

MOB-REPELLING FIRE BEACONS
Keep your desert oasis safe from mobs by placing a few strategic campfires around the perimeter.

EXTERIOR

Inspired by mysterious desert pyramids, I have hidden my base deep beneath the surface, only accessible to those who know how to find it. Unwanted visitors will fall victim to my cunning traps!

TREE FARM
Grow all the wood your base needs indoors.

LIBRARY
I love old books. They're filled with answers to ancient mysteries.

ROYAL BEDCHAMBER
This is where the pharaoh's mummified remains reside, preserved in their stone sarcophagus for eternity.

DEFENSIVE MAZE
Unprepared adventurers are sure to get lost among the dead ends, dark nooks and hostile mobs.

WATERFALL EXIT

DEFENSIVE PARKOUR COURSE
Hot lava, scary jumps and narrow ledges make this parkour course incredibly challenging.

CRAFTING AREA

INTERIOR

BUILD TECHNIQUES

Ancient civilizations look exactly that – ancient! Making the base look old was a challenge, but I have a few tricks tucked up my sleeve that help make my creation look 3,000 years old.

ENTRANCE AND ATRIUM

Raised high above the ground, the grand entrance holds the atrium and a large pool of water. Flowing into the entrance is a waterfall that hides the secret entrance to the tomb.

WATERFALL ENTRANCE

The waterfall entrance consists of a hole in the back wall, through which a stream of water flows. To reach the base you must swim up the waterfall and into the hole. Follow the water as it descends, until you emerge underground.

smooth quartz

red sandstone

prismarine brick

BLOCK CHOICES

Since this base is in the desert, I used a variety of sandstone blocks for the foundations, with red sandstone for contrast. I also used smooth quartz, prismarine bricks and orange glazed terracotta to create decorative details. To light up the base, I placed braziers along the outer perimeter.

orange glazed terracotta

sandstone

SECRET BASE

The base area itself is hidden deep beneath the lava-filled parkour course and is only accessible via a secret door at the end of the parkour course. To reveal the secret door, you need to solve a redstone puzzle by pulling levers in the correct order. Once solved, a hidden mechanism will reveal the passage to the base.

FIRE-BEARING STATUES

The statues are constructed from a combination of sandstone and chiseled sandstone, and have campfires nestled in their hand. The mouths of the statues are made from stair blocks and the eyes from buttons.

PILLARS AND RIVERS

I constructed the pillars from a variety of blocks. Using different blocks allowed me to add some fun detail – stairs, buttons and fences help to break up the smooth line of the full blocks and add elements of interest. The rivers are made using stair blocks and numerous buckets of water.

USEFUL FEATURES

Who goes in and who comes out of the ancient tomb is my main concern. This isn't a public space! Getting in is no walk in the park, but getting out again has its hazards too. I've worked too hard to risk my reseach being stolen!

BEDCHAMBER

My bedchamber is located just below the entombed mummy. If it was comfortable enough for ancient civilizations, it's comfortable enough for me!

LADDER PARKOUR

Parkour isn't everyone's game. To get through the parkour course, adventurers need to be savvy ladder-hoppers. One small slip on these rungs and the intruder will drop to their doom.

INDOOR FARMING

I wanted my base to be completely self-sufficient. An indoor farm will keep me well supplied with food. Crops will grow as long as there's a light source, so I went ahead and planted the seeds, placed some torches and waited for my crops to grow.

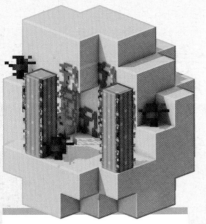

SECRET EXIT

A secret exit back to the surface is hidden in the bedchamber's wardobe. Hopefully I'll never need to use this escape route, but having it in place helps me sleep at night.

DAYLIGHT DOORWAY

The secret door to access my base is operated by a redstone puzzle. I decided to time-lock the entrance with a daylight sensor, opening the doors during the day and sealing them at night. Tomb raiders who lose track of time will be stumped!

INSTRUCTIONS

Using the images provided, follow steps 1–7 to build your very own daylight sensor doorway. It can be as far below ground as you like, just build your signal ladder up until you reach the surface.

1

Build a 6x10 plinth to use as the base of your doorway and add a long step.

2

Place the 2 redstone repeaters and 6 redstone dusts at both of the shorter ends as shown. Set the redstone repeater to 2 ticks.

3

Build a 4-block bridge above each of the redstone repeaters, then add 3 more redstone dust on each bridge.

4

Place 6 sticky pistons in an L-shape beside each of the bridges.

5

Place 4 red sandstones touching the sticky pistons. Above your structure, build another platform and place 10 redstone dusts in the pattern shown.

Signal ladder

6

In the far corner, build a signal ladder to the surface and place a daylight sensor at the top. To build a signal ladder, place blocks in a rising zigzag shape with a redstone dust and a redstone torch on each block. Add 4 glowstone blocks.

7

Style your doorway in your chosen theme. I used sandstone and red sandstone to match the ancient tomb theme.

THE LOFTY LAB

For years I have worked tirelessly in the name of science. Mixing ingredients and enchanting tools has been my life's work. And now, after many days and nights cooped up inside, I'm pleased to announce my greatest invention yet – the Lofty Lab! The miracle of science has, once again, provided solutions to my problems! Take a look at some of the special features I've included in my floating laboratory.

PROPELLERS

BALLONETS

NETHER PORTAL
A floating, isolated Nether portal provides unlimited access to the essential resources needed in my work.

DR. ATTICUS SPARK
Traveling Inventor

POTIONS ROOM

WINDMILL

LIGHTS
A well-lit airship is a safe airship. No mobs will be spawning on my base.

EXTERIOR

19

With so much machinery, going steampunk felt like the natural theme for my floating lab. It fits perfectly with the huge air balloons. I completed the look with a few pieces of advanced technology.

FUMIGATION HUT

A lab is not complete without a fumigation hut. Though not functional, this chimney is one of the finishing details that turns this from a regular base into an *epic* base.

LIBRATORY

Raised high above the ground, the library-laboratory is the core of my base. It's packed with bookshelves, an enchanting table and, of course, an anvil. I lovingly refer to it as my libratory.

VICTORIAN ARCHITECTURE

Victorian architecture is a fantastic reference source for steampunk enthusiasts. This wooden frame, lined with smooth stone edges and a polished stone facade, is almost identical to those found in the late nineteenth century. Half-timbering designs were characteristic of the era.

CURTAINS

Stack banners one on top of the other to create a patterned curtain.

POTIONS LAB

BLOCK CHOICES

Once I had decided on a floating laboratory and airship, I selected blocks that fit with my desired theme. Colors associated with steampunk commonly include black, brown, cream, dark green and dark red, so I chose blocks that worked with this color palette. I had to include barrels as its metal bindings fit perfectly with industrial themes. I find the result very pleasing.

barrel   anvil   green concrete   white concrete   cobblestone

LEVELS

If you're a stockpiler like me, finding space for all your tools, equipment and inventions can be a struggle. We can all benefit from some extra storage. Consider building extra levels to your base. The sky's the limit to what you can now accommodate.

GIANT MUSHROOMS

It can be a challenge to fit color into an industrial theme. Don't let that stop you! Use flora to add some natural colors. These giant mushrooms are an explosion of color and contrast nicely against the exterior buildings. There are other fantastic options too, like the huge fungus found in the Nether.

21

USEFUL FEATURES

Although I have everything I need up here on my floating paradise, I do occasionally venture down to solid ground. When duty calls, I use my small airship to travel with haste.

AIRSHIP EXPRESS

This invention here is my small airship for speedy travel. It shares a lot of the same technology as my floating lab. I colored it green so I can disguise it among the trees while I'm on the ground.

ENGINE FURNACE

The airship's engine is a campfire covered by a trapdoor. Pull the lever to release the smoke into the balloon and power the airship. It won't go anywhere but it will look impressive!

QUARTERDECK

Every airship needs a quarterdeck. Here I've used a lectern as the captain's wheel.

SYMMETRY

Key to a good airship design is symmetry. My top tip is to create the outline for the ship first, and then focus your attention on one side. When you're happy with how it looks, copy the design to complete the other side of the airship.

BALLOONS

Layering the balloons was the hardest challenge. It required some extensive work, but I'm pleased with the results. Add a few details with trapdoors, slabs and fences for detailing, and we're left with a pretty awesome tethered balloon!

AIRSHIP DESIGN

Airships can be as small or as large as you like. Simply pick your favorite design and scale it to the desired size. This airship is compact, with just a quarterdeck, engine and storage room – perfect for speedy missions.

BALLONETS

The ballonets are very similar to the large balloons, though smaller and more rounded. These can fit in narrow spaces without obstructing the view of the airship. Plus, they look amazing! They're the perfect thematic decoration to fill empty space.

STORAGE SPACE

Small airships can still have plenty of storage. I keep a hollow space below the deck to store a few large chests. It's always handy to have a few emergency supplies nearby.

PROPELLERS

The propellers add a touch of modernity to the steampunk theme. Made from wool, buttons and trapdoors, they may not be functional but they're definitely thematic. These propellers contrast nicely against the balloons and ballonets.

THE SUNKEN ESTATE

Lost deep beneath the ocean's surface for many years, the Sunken Estate was the home of my ancestors. I have dedicated my youth to its rediscovery, combing through countless archives for any reference to the long-lost palace. A recent breakthrough has finally led me to my ancestral home, but years of neglect had left it in ruin. My latest project has been to restore it to its former glory.

MARINE OBSERVATION GLASS

KELP GARDENS
The biggest challenge of an underwater base is keeping these detestable kelp gardens in check. Honestly, they never stop growing!

TRANSFER TUNNELS
These long and elegant tunnels lead through darkness. Marine life does not require much light to see.

MARIA TRENCH
Deep-Sea Explorer

DROWNED MOBS

GRAND DOME & SUB-DOMES
Broad and expansive, these majestic domes are fit for a palace.

GRAND STAINED GLASS WINDOWS

SAND DUNES

EXTERIOR

BUILD TECHNIQUES

DOME STRUCTURE

The circular structure of domes has been an architectural challenge since prehistoric times. Not to worry! I've provided some helpful outlines for you to try below.

Though impressive in their own right, the domes and sub-domes serve as windows into the ocean. The estate has become a hot spot for local flora and fauna, which can be observed through the large expanse of glass.

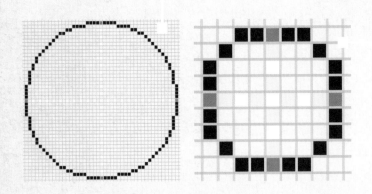

GO FULL CIRCLE

These outlines are a great starting point for a dome. Begin with this structure and scale it once you're comfortable with the shape.

DOME

Did you know that domes are super-strong structures? They don't even need internal support beams.

GRAND DOME

As the pinnacle of my deep-sea base, the grand dome houses the Great Hall and has been designed to be both awe-inspiring and imposing. Built with crystal-clear glass blocks, prismarine and quartz, the dome blends into the ocean, its colors mirroring its aquatic setting.

SKYLIGHTS

CONNECTOR

Each transfer tunnel and sub-dome is supported by connector structures, adding to the scale and overall strength of the Sunken Estate.

DECO STYLE

I used an art deco theme for my base. With lots of small windows, spiraling archways and long, soaring columns, these domes look a lot like skyscrapers – or, as I like to call them, surfacescrapers. Place sea lanterns on the exterior to light up the ocean and its marine life. How's that for a view?

prismarine   dark prismarine

ARCHWAY

Archway designs are essential to this build. Try building one in Creative mode to decide what design you like most before starting any major construction work.

BLOCK CHOICES

Inspired by the deep-sea greens and blues, I selected prismarine and dark prismarine blocks for my base structure. I also used a great many glass blocks, which serve as windows into the ocean. There's also a lot of kelp but I usually spend my time removing it, instead of adding it!

Underwater constructions face serious flooding issues. Try using sponges – they are a fantastic way to drain water from your build. Simply use a furnace to dry them out when you need more.

USEFUL FEATURES

I want my base to be a home for all, including the local marine life. Any fish that swim near the Sunken Estate are more than welcome to stay as long as they like in my fish-friendly aquarium. Come and take a seat.

AQUARIUM

My aquarium has been built to house fish of all species, with coral reef homes, kelp gardens and sand trenches. Visitors at the Sunken Estate are encouraged to spend some time here to appreciate the diversity of marine life.

TILING

Tiling is a great way to add distinction to your build. Simple, two-block patterns are easy to create and highly effective.

CORALS

Corals add fantastic color to the prismarine base. You can place them in the aquarium or the hallway – they don't need water to survive.

TROPICAL FISH

Fancy having your very own tropical fish paradise? Make sure to build your base in a warm water biome.

DROWNED MOB FARM

The Sunken Estate seems to attract drowned mobs like a magnet, so I've built a drowned mob farm to tackle the issue. Rewards include experience orbs, tridents and gold ingots!

INSTRUCTIONS

Using the images provided, follow steps 1–10 to build your very own drowned mob farm. This farm is 5x5 blocks wide and 12 blocks tall. I highly recommend building the farm in Creative mode before adding it to your base in Survival.

1

Dig a hole in the seabed 6 blocks deep, 5x5 wide. This will be the main chamber.

2

Place a trapdoor in the center of the hole, an inner ring of building blocks and an outer ring of magma blocks.

3

Place 4 turtle eggs and 4 trapdoors on top of the inner ring as shown.

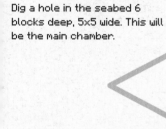

4

Build a glass tunnel 4 blocks high and 3x3 wide above the inner ring. Block the tunnel at the top.

5

Place slabs in a ring above the glass tunnel and fill the hole with a water bucket.

6

Build a 2-block-tall glass tunnel on top of the slabs, place the villager inside and enclose it within a dome. Place water sources on every block above the magma – that's 82 buckets!

10

Place a hopper, chest and rail cart as shown.

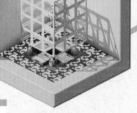

COLLECTIONS ROOM

To use the drowned mob farm, take the ladder down to the collections room and then sit back and wait for the chest to fill up with valuable loot.

7

Open the first trapdoor and dig out a space below the main chamber measuring 5x5 wide and 6 blocks deep. Add a pillar and ladder. This will be the collections room.

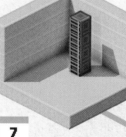

8

Create a block around the perimeter.

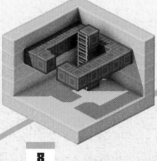

9

Place the rails and powered rails as shown. Add a redstone torch below the powered rails.

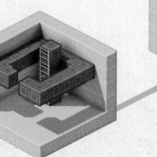

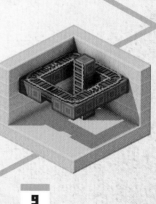

FENRIR'S TOOTH

Welcome aboard my ship, *Fenrir's Tooth*! These decks have taken me across the deep blue seas, from the heart of civilization to the farthest and darkest corners of the realm. Armed with a veritable arsenal of artillery, we bring the fight to the mobs and banish evildoers from the land. Keep an eye on the horizon and listen for the sound of the cannon announcing my arrival.

WOLF HEAD
Strike fear into the hearts of your foes with an intimidating figurehead.

BRAZIERS

GUNHILDA FENRIR
Viking Berserker

CROW'S NEST
Always keep an eagle-eyed ally posted in the lookout box to warn the crew about imminent threats. The drowned know no peace.

FLAG

EMERALD WOLF

ARTILLERY CANNON
A watery grave awaits the poor souls facing this powerhouse. If you thought creepers were explosive, you haven't been introduced to my TNT-fueled friend.

OARS

EXTERIOR

31

*F*enrir's Tooth is a formidable ship, easily the mightiest in the realm. The strength of its structure and the ferocity of its prow makes defeating this floating fortress nigh on impossible. My crew consider it unbeatable.

BOAT RIBS

The boat ribs set the scale and outline for the ship. It can be as large or as small as you desire, but I strongly recommend deciding how big you want your base before starting construction. It will save a lot of frustration later on.

PROW

The prow is the forward-most part of the ship that cuts through water. I added the figurehead of a wolf to honor my favorite mob and to strike fear into the hearts of my foes.

BILLOWING SAILS

To make the sails billow in the wind, I used a combination of stairs, slabs and regular blocks. Arranging the blocks in layers gives the impression of them having caught a gale.

CUTAWAY

This cutaway sets the frame for my base. From side to side it is 41 blocks wide, and from end to end it is 170 blocks long. It's large for a ship, but small for a base.

STORAGE CABIN

Optimizing space is essential for compact bases. This small storage cabin on the main deck is filled with a little bit of everything so I can resupply quickly – trouble can strike at any moment, so I must be prepared. The bulk of the supplies remain below deck.

UNEQUAL SIDES

I rotated the hay bales as I placed them. The uneven sides give the thatching a rough look.

BUNK BEDS

Space is at a premium aboard the ship. I packed the crew into bunk bed dorms to fit as many people in as possible. It builds camaraderie among the sailors.

MAP TABLE

I've installed a large map table in the battle room, with detailed notes on every corner of the realm. I keep cartography tables at hand in case I need to copy a section of the map for an expedition inland.

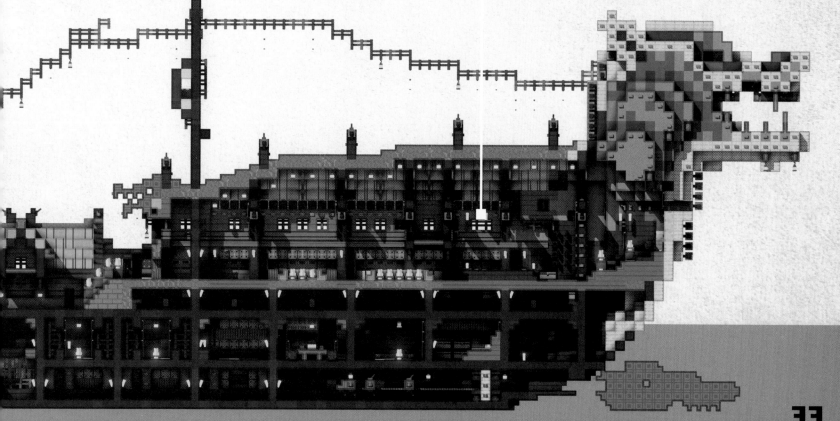

USEFUL FEATURES

Every element of my ship has been carefully thought out, striking a fine balance between elegance and powerhouse. The cannon is my pièce de résistance. As long as I have this cannon, I am unstoppable.

CROSSBEAMS

The jutting crossbeams that roof my ship fit with the Viking longship theme I've chosen. The X-shape can be done in numerous styles, so experiment and find what works best for you.

BRAZIERS

The drowned are naturally drawn toward the ship, and its wooden hull makes it vulnerable to their attacks. Placing braziers will help keep their numbers down – and your ship leak-free.

THATCHED ROOFING

Hay bales are *Fenrir's Tooth's* crowning glory. Though they are a potential fire hazard, the ship's masts, as the tallest points of the ship, provide protection from lightning strikes.

THRONE

Don't be mistaken – *Fenrir's Tooth* is not simply a ship. It is a castle, a palace and a symbol of status. And as such, it would be incomplete without an imposing throne room. *My* throne room.

EMERALD WOLF

The emerald wolf guards the entrance to the throne room and acts as strong reminder of my status to those I summon.

ARTILLERY CANNON

I built the cannon to give me an edge in battle – not to blow up my own ship! There's a lot of TNT packed into this build so you better watch out or you'll be missing fingers by the time we're done!

INSTRUCTIONS

Using the images and block key provided, follow steps 1–6 to build your very own TNT cannon. I strongly recommend testing this build before placing it in your base. Highly explosive!

1

Create the frame for your cannon as shown.

2

Add 9 redstone repeaters, a redstone torch and 10 redstone dusts. Set the lower redstone repeaters to 4 ticks.

3

Place 6 more wooden blocks on the upper level alongside the redstone repeaters.

4

Place 6 dispensers facing upward above the new wooden blocks and create a platform around it. Then place a slab, 2 wooden blocks, a staircase and a dispenser as shown. Add a redstone torch below the dispenser.

5

Place two stairs touching the redstone torch and the opposing wooden block. Then add a cauldron, grindstone and button as shown.

6

Clad the cannon by placing trapdoors on either side between the upper dispenser and the cauldron, and fill the gap with water. Fill all the dispensers with TNT and press the button to fire the cannon.

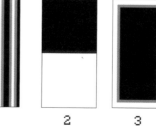

BLOCK CHOICES

I looked to the Nordic Viking longships for inspiration designing my warship. Just like *Fenrir's Tooth*, Viking ships were designed for long-term living, as they sailed on stormy seas. I used spruce logs, dark oak planks, hay bales and iron blocks to make this design.

hay bale

dark oak planks

iron

spruce log

SHIELDS

The longship is completed with the addition of shields along its grab rail. I used a combination of banners and stairs to imitate shields and dressed them with banners using the patterns below.

1   2   3

THE EXCHANGE

Watch your step! This is an active dig site. My base has been designed as a fully functioning field research station. I want to find out everything I can about the structures of the Overworld and those who built them. If you need to decipher an illager code or duplicate a rare map, you've come to the right place! I'm all set up to delve deep into the long-lost histories of Minecraft.

COMMUNITY
A village cartographer revealed the location of this End portal to me. A trading community has sprung up around the portal, trading in resources from exotic dimensions.

FLOWERING FOLIAGE

LILY PAD PATHS

KAT SEEKER
Wilderness Explorer

SUPPORT STRUCTURES
I built wooden platforms into the sides of the pyramid. They serve as observation and research rooms.

ETERNAL FLAME
This flame has never been extinguished. My research has determined it must be burning netherrack imported through the portal.

REDSTONE ALTAR
How the ancients tracked the passing of time is a mystery. I'm experimenting with these redstone altars to find out more.

REMNANT MEMORIAL
Skeleton heads lay on the floor when I first arrived at this village. Unsure what to do with them, I created these statues as a memorial for fallen adventurers everywhere.

BUILD TECHNIQUES

Constructing a research site in the middle of a jungle has its challenges. Thankfully, there was no shortage of wooden logs to build with. I reserved stone blocks for the pyramid so that it is clearly the oldest-looking building on my dig site.

EYE OF ENDER
When I found the End portal it was missing a few eyes of ender. I tracked down a few endermen and quickly found eyes to replace those that were missing.

STEPWELL
The base of the pyramid builds downward like a stepwell toward the End portal. These tapering walls fit perfectly with the pyramid structure. I tell visiting players that the steps were built by the "original builders" when they were searching for water.

STATUE
Old stone statues survive the test of time better than any other material. Perfect for making a base look aged.

LOCATION, LOCATION, LOCATION
To find an End portal you need to locate a stronghold. Strongholds naturally generate and can be found using eyes of ender. There must have once been a stronghold here.

AZTECS AND MAYANS
I took my inspiration from the Aztec and Mayan civilizations. They built fascinating pyramids, temples, palaces and residences. There's lots to be inspired by!

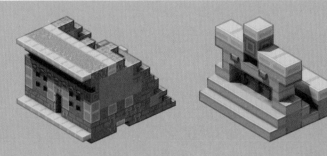

SUPPORTS

Minor details should never be overlooked – they add character to the build. I designed these supports as they fit with my Aztec and Mayan theme. If an area was too sparse, I put a few of these in place.

OAK, SPRUCE OR ACACIA

With so many trees around, I had an abundance of wooden logs to build with. I grabbed my axe and started chopping. This cabin uses all three wood types.

TRADING

Your villagers will trade all the resources you need – if you can protect them. They're helpless in a fight so you better be careful that no mobs break in!

USEFUL FEATURES

BARE NECESSITIES

Villagers need food, shelter and employment to survive. Every village must provide these three requirements. It's up to you to make sure they have them!

MEMORIALS

The skeleton heads of lost adventurers were dotted around my research site during construction. I used them to create a special memorial so that they will never be forgotten again.

STREETLIGHTS

As villagers won't defend themselves, I've taken additional measures to safeguard them from hostile mobs. These street-lights illuminate all dark corners and keep mobs from spawning within my walls.

THRIVING ECONOMY

Tailor the job market to your base's needs. Villagers choose jobs according to available job blocks. Need a farmer? Create a composter. What about a map? Craft yourself a cartographer's table!

STILT HOUSES

Need more crop-growing space? Stilted houses will maximize the available pasturelands, with the added bonus of keeping villagers safe.

TRADE ROUTES

Establish trade routes along the river to trade with nearby players. Nether and End resources are in high demand!

SOURCING SETTLERS

Attention all survivalists! Building a thriving village has its challenges but none so challenging as bringing villagers to your new home. Lure a villager from a nearby village into a minecart and bring them "home" with you.

VORACIOUS VILLAGERS

Include some basic crops for villagers to farm. Placing a composter will get a nearby unemployed villager to look after the crops for you. Villagers will farm these crops to breed and produce more villagers.

SQUIRRELED AWAY

Aerial walkways are great for expanding. Inviting your friends to join you? Just build treehouses and join them with walkways.

CRYPTIC ENGRAVINGS

I engraved the pyramid floor with cryptic drawings. I found similar patterns in an old book and I decided they would look perfect in my base. I wonder what they mean.

GOOD DEEDS, GOOD REPUTATION

Villagers love to gossip so be aware that any good deeds – and bad ones – will affect your reputation and the trading prices.

BARRIERS

Don't forget to add some barriers! It's a long way down to the ground.

THE CUBE

Where are we, you ask? Well, there's no easy answer to that question. I didn't have much control over where I landed, as I had no intention of landing in the first place. Suffice it to say we are very far from my home and very near to yours. Please, take a look around! My dream is to one day fly this ship into space to discover who and what lives among the stars.

OVERGROWN VEGETATION
The city seems to have been abandoned long ago. Look, nature has overtaken most buildings.

CRUMBLED RUINS
I swear these buildings were already damaged when I crashed here.

STEVEN STARGAZER

Xenoarchaeologist

THE CUBE'S MAW
Access to the Cube is via a small gap in the force field.

LOOK TO THE STARS
The countless square stars in the night sky inspired my build. Who lives up there? And do they also travel in cube shaped ships? I like to think they do.

RADIANT LIGHTING
The natural glow of the Cube acts as a beacon, attracting mobs from far and wide.

TOXIC EXCLUSION ZONE
The area surrounding the Cube has a noxious glow. It looks to have been flooded by a poisonous gas.

BUILD TECHNIQUES

M y alien-inspired designs are all the rage. Look at all those smooth, straight lines and sharp edges. Honestly, is a better aesthetic even possible?

TESTING LAB

I've created my very own lab with individual holding chambers for mobs and blocks. Testing is already underway on some blocks. Did you know you can create diorite blocks by stonecutting two cobblestone and two nether quartz?

PROPERTIES

This chamber is where I test the capabilities of individual blocks I find in the local biome. Some blocks can transmit redstone signals; some change into new blocks when placed in a furnace. Some blocks can even be combined together. Better get testing!

REINFORCED HOLDING CHAMBERS

MOB MUSEUM

I'm fascinated by the wonderful animals and mobs that roam the realm. I had to gather some samples. This here is my mob museum featuring all the mobs I've collected so far – as you can see, I'm still missing a few. Not to worry, I'll soon catch them all.

MOB EXAMINATION GALLERY

CIRCUIT BOARD DESIGN

Alien technology is extremely advanced ... I think. This has inspired my build design. My entire base looks like an endless grooved circuit board.

NATURAL LIGHTING

Even alien bases need lighting to stay safe from spawning mobs. Sticking with my futuristic theme, I have included natural lighting around the base with glowstones, warped wood and nether brick stairs. The purple-green colors work perfectly together.

MOLTEN CORE

Lava encased in glass still produces its fluid, flickering particle effect. I encased the lava core so that observers feel the engine's raw power.

PURPLE PANES

I've used a lot of obsidian and red nether brick building this base. To give these dark colors contrast, I made good use of purple panes. These windows look fantastic and give off a strong futuristic vibe.

CORE CUBE

The engine that fuels the Cube.

ENCASEMENT

I built the engine using obsidian, the most durable of blocks available, to reduce the chances of it getting damaged. It might be unnecessary, but I don't want to risk all of this lava escaping and burning down my base! Pro tip: take extra precautionary measures against fire hazards!

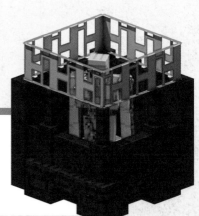

The Cube is unlike any other fortress. Virtually impregnable, the vessel has every defense system available. From patrolling guards to energized force fields and obsidian foundations, getting into my base is a life-threatening and time-consuming challenge.

LAVA-CURTAIN FORCE FIELD

The huge force field that protects the Cube has additional security measures. Look closely and you will see there's a lava curtain in place between two glass panel walls – a little extra protection against unwanted guests.

REINFORCED STRUCTURE

The Cube is built using obsidian and iron, making it extremely difficult to penetrate. Trespassers had better be well prepared if they intend on getting past these walls – it will take more than a stone pickaxe!

NARROW ENTRY

The only way into my base is through a narrow 2x2 entryway in the center of a force field – not for the faint-hearted. You'll need an elytra, fireworks and a high vantage point to get in.

PUPPET SOLDIERS

My loyal golem soldiers patrol the area, chasing off pillagers and bringing home new specimens for my mob museum.

AUTOMATIC DOORWAY

I endeavored to make my base the most advanced in the realm. Even stepping through doorways visitors will be impressed with the level of futuristic technology. These automatic doorways are but a small element of the redstone mechanisms hidden within. I suppose I can show you how to make them ...

INSTRUCTIONS

Using the images provided, follow steps 1–7 to build your very own automatic doorway. You can style the doors however you like – simply replace the quartz blocks with your block of choice.

1

Start by creating an 8x5 rectangle as shown above.

2

Then, on the shorter sides, build a second level and add redstone dust and redstone repeaters as shown.

3

Add a third level on the shorter sides and place more redstone dust and redstone repeaters as shown.

4

Fill in the third level with quartz blocks, keeping the short sides clear.

5

Create a new fourth level, adding 10 quartz blocks in an X-shaped format with 2 redstone torches on opposite ends as shown.

6

Place 2 more construction blocks and 4 sticky pistons as shown, then place stone pressure plates across either side to activate the door mechanism.

7

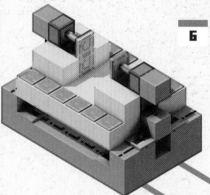

Place 4 quartz blocks on the 4 sticky pistons and then design the doorway to fit your theme. I used buttons, stairs and quartz to fit my futuristic theme.

CRUMBLING RUINS

Give your base character with some background structures. Crumbling ruins are easy to create: just build a normal structure and detonate some TNT.

STREETLIGHTS

Streetlights might seem like a boring construction but dotted into the background of a ruined city, they are exactly the sort of minor detail that elevates a build to epic new heights.

GLISTENING ICE PALACE

High above the clouds and hidden among the snowy peaks sits the Glistening Ice Palace. Constructed out of ice blocks hand-carved from ancient glaciers, my palace's brilliance is second to none. Only the most arduous of explorers have any hope of reaching my base. If the freezing winds don't stop them in their tracks, my snow golems will pelt them away with snowballs.

FROZEN FORUM

OUTPOST
Manned by snow golems, outposts surround the base.

TEMPLE RUN
Rich white quartz bridges connect each of the structures together.

ALDUR BLUETOUCH
Frost King

SILK TOUCH
I carved these ice blocks using tools enchanted with silk touch.

AMPHITHEATER
Light sources can be problematic for ice builds. Harness the natural light with open-air venues.

DOCKS

SIGNALING BEACON

EXTERIOR

BUILD TECHNIQUES

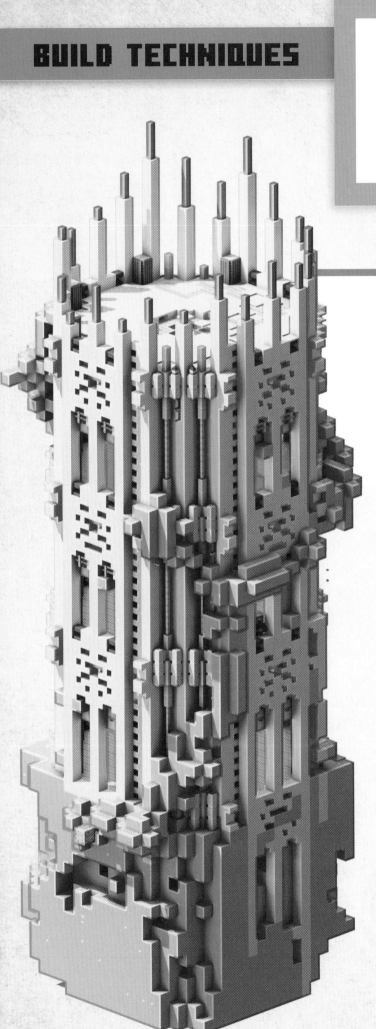

My base was inspired by the fantastical tales of Elven cities and hidden havens. These majestic towers, complete with grand windows and snowy surfaces, are eerily wonderful and ageless.

RAGGED SCULPTING

To create this spiraling ice effect, collect ice blocks using a silk touch-enchanted pickaxe and place the ice around your build by hand. This is a challenging task, so make sure to wait until you've finished the main structure before starting it.

TREE

With an abundance of blue and white blocks, I decided the base needed a spot of color. Trees are perfect for piercing the scene with splashes of green.

ELVEN DESIGN

Elven buildings usually blend seamlessly into nature. A great way to achieve this is to use natural blocks in your design. When combined with ice, snow and water, pale birch wood fences and snow-like quartz give the buildings a magical, timeless effect commonly associated with elves.

BLOCK CHOICES

I firmly believe quartz is essential to any icy biome structure. It's the perfect substitute for snow and it won't melt in the sun. I used every form of quartz in this base. I then selected birch items to fit my Elven theme.

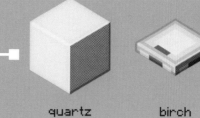

quartz

birch trapdoors

birch stairs

birch fence

BESPOKE ARCHITECTURE

Varying the sizes and shapes of towers gives you the opportunity to add new and creative features. I built this tower to house my bespoke semi-automatic snowman farm. I didn't stop there – I also designed special spaces for housing and entertainment.

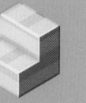

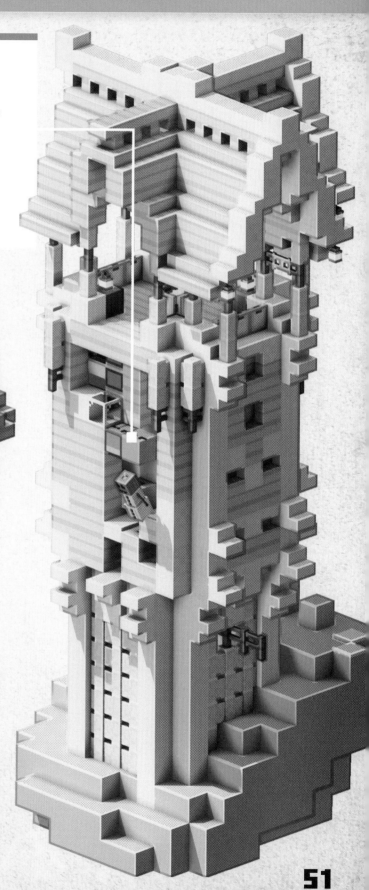

DOORWAYS, ALCOVES & PASSAGES

A frozen sheet of ice is a dangerous canvas to work on. I would know – it's exactly what I started with. I dotted these structures around my build to avoid digging too deep and causing the ice to collapse. These structures are useful, creative finishes for giving your base seemingly endless depth.

OUTPOST TOWER

Small-scale towers are brilliant for giving a base additional depth. These narrow and super-simple builds can be placed anywhere. They are so simple in fact that you can build them all along your base's perimeter.

Building ice structures does pose its challenges. The most frustrating is preventing the ice from melting. Light sources wreak havoc on the ice, but luckily I know a thing or two about building with ice.

ICE SPIKES

Water sources naturally freeze when exposed directly to the sky in cold biomes. A very handy trick to create ice spikes is to climb up high with buckets of water and place them in your desired locations. They will freeze naturally into spikes. No ice carving required!

LIGHT SOURCES

The bane of all ice builds is lighting. It's just so difficult to brighten an ice base when almost all light sources cause ice blocks to melt. Alas, it is not all bad news! Every light source has a limit to how close ice can be before it melts. Campfires and torches won't melt any ice blocks that are more than 3 blocks away.

SOUL FIRE LIGHTS

Not all light sources are problematic. Soul fire torches and soul fire lamps have lower light levels and won't melt ice or snow. Visit the Nether to collect the soul soil needed.

OPEN-AIR VENUES

Amphitheaters are a clever way to avoid the lighting issue – by not lighting it at all! There are lots of open-air buildings you could try, like conservatories, verandas and gazebos. Watch out for the mobs that spawn at night when it gets dark.

DISTANCE

Of course, every base needs some lighting. Each light source has a light level that diminishes the farther away you are. The campfire in this chamber is just far enough away to not melt the ice blocks on the outside.

INSTRUCTIONS

Use the layer-by-layer images provided to build your very own snow golem farm. It's a complicated build so make sure you focus on one layer at a time. Remember, you're going to need a lot of snow and carved pumpkins for your snow golems!

SNOW GOLEM SOLDIERS

An unfortunate consequence of a poorly lit base is an endless flow of pesky mobs. Some might consider this a deal-breaker, but not I. For every problem, there is a solution. In this case, an army of formidable snow golems! Good luck getting into my base with these guards blocking the way.

1

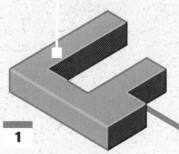

Start by building an F-shaped base layer as shown using normal blocks.

2

Add a second layer of blocks and place 3 redstone repeaters and 6 redstone dust in the positions shown.

3

Stack 2 pistons in the center in front of the 2 redstone repeaters. Then place a third sticky piston opposite the first redstone repeater.

4

Build a third layer with blocks. Add a sticky piston above the single piston, then place a glass block and a slab as shown.

5

Place 2 redstone repeaters and 3 redstone dust on the third layer and then add 2 slabs, 2 blocks and a dispenser as shown.

180°

6

Rotate your view and add normal blocks as shown. Place a redstone repeater and redstone dust on the slabs, then add a glass block and 2 redstone dust above the dispenser.

7

Place stairs and normal blocks flanking the dispenser as shown. Above the glass block, add a redstone repeater, slab and redstone dust.

180°

8

Add 2 downward-facing sticky pistons alongside the top glass block.

9

Encase your build in the style of your choosing.

Test your build by placing a carved pumpkin or a jack o'lantern in the dispenser and two blocks of snow below the downward-facing pistons. When you're ready, press the button to activate the redstone repeaters.

BASE IN ACTION

Welcome back to the Exchange! The gang have assembled at Kat Seeker's base after hearing the reverberating clang of the great bell. The pyramid has fallen into disrepair and invaders are attempting to break through its defenses. The Twelve have rallied to its defense, each member throwing their weight to bring the base back to functioning order.

Rita's splash potions are proving devastating to the zombie hordes.

Kat will defend her villagers at all costs. She'll jump off a building if she has to!

Atticus is brandishing his latest invention – the Blade of Sharpness!
Cornelius Luckless is standing well away from the fray. He won't get caught this time!
Flint Scree is running into the thick of battle, swinging his great hammer with deadly precision.

THE SHIMMERING HOARD

Welcome to my treasure trove! Do not – I repeat – DO NOT disturb the dragon. He hasn't budged in centuries. He's my most loyal subject, and the protector of the Shimmering Hoard. Forged by the fires at the very heart of the mountain, this hoard is the envy of kings. We're heading far below ground so watch your head and don't forget to bring a torch!

MOUNTAIN PETS
Or as you know them, bats.

SUPER STATUES
These statues have beacons contained within. Visitors feel empowered by their nearby presence.

FLINT SCREE
Forge Lord

MINE CARTS
These carts bring an endless supply of coal to the forge.

TREASURE TROVE
Lavish, extravagant and guarded by a bone dragon; visitors will have to pinch themselves to be convinced the treasure is real.

SMELTING STATION
The automatic smelting station will smelt the metal from any ore.

LAVA LAKE
Lava streams down into the lake below. The orange glow of the lava is enhanced with magma blocks, found in the Nether.

BUILD TECHNIQUES

The mountain...it speaks to me. It tells me what it wants to be, and I follow as commanded. I have painstakingly hand-chiseled every detail of this kingdom, and there's not one block out of place.

NATURAL FEATURES

Always take advantage of the Overworld's raw form. This was a naturally formed cavern. I simply expanded it – a few blocks here and a few blocks there – and converted it into this grand hall. TNT will help speed up the process.

SUPPORT STRUCTURES

Subterranean bases often have huge caverns and tall ceilings. Consider adding support structures to make your base look more realistic. Design a column and arch you like and then install them around your base.

NO BURNT TOES

If you want a lava lake, you're going to need to build some raised pathways to get around. You could combine these with the support structures to save space.

ARCHITECTURAL STYLE

Subterranean bases are quite popular so I wanted to give mine some unique features. I built a double-lip ledge using staircases and gave all the chambers flat roofs. It gives my base character.

LAVA FOUNTAIN

To all you survivalists out there: redirect lava springs throughout the mountain to flow into the core of your base. Impress your friends by adding valves, starting and stopping the flow of water with the flick of a switch.

DEBRIS PROTECTION

Finishing touches make the difference between good and great bases. I've installed some overhead protection to catch falling debris — just like you would find in a real-world cave.

BLOCK CHOICE

Safety first! The Shimmering Hoard is made predominantly out of fireproof blocks. Why? Because of all the lava, of course! My main blocks were cobblestone and nether brick, but you will also find a lot of details made with gold blocks and grindstones.

gold block

nether brick

grindstone

cobblestone

SWAMP WATER

Tired of always using the same clear blue water? Go and check out a swamp biome. They produce a gray-green colored water that turns pale yellow when you're submerged. As you can see, I built this base below a swamp biome just for this cool effect.

USEFUL FEATURES

Digging mines into the heart of the mountain has provided me with extraordinary quantities of ores. My smelting station is of immeasurable value, processing all my resources with minimal effort.

MINE SHAFT STRUCTURE

There are a lot of ways to make a mine shaft. I built this one with a spiral staircase and a mine-cart shaft. Going down is easy but getting resources back up is a challenge. I created a hidden cart system using powered rails to ensure loaded carts make it back to the exit. It's a long way to walk, but this way I know my resources are waiting at the top.

LAVA LIGHTING

Who needs natural light when you have radiant light! Flowing lava contained in glass will give the base a raw, natural glow.

SUPER STATUES

One of the greatest displays of wealth in Minecraft are beacons. They use a *lot* of rare resources, but they are totally worth the perks they offer. I built my beacons into the heads of the statues at the entrance to my base so that upon entering my domain, visitors will run faster, jump higher and feel stronger.

AUTOMATIC SMELTING STATION

Processing mined ores is an extremely time-consuming process. This smelting station is fully automatic – simply place your ores into the chests and return later to collect ingots and experience points. Don't forget to keep a steady supply of fuel!

INSTRUCTIONS

Using the images provided, follow steps 1–7 to build your very own automatic smelting station. It is essential that you place the hoppers correctly for this build. For ease, crouch when placing blocks alongside utility blocks.

1

Start by creating a 12x3 plinth with 2 protruding blocks as shown.

2

Place 6 furnaces in a line with 6 hoppers feeding into them.

3

Place 14 more hoppers, with 6 hoppers feeding into the blast furnaces and 8 hoppers feeding toward the right-hand side.

4

Place 6 chests on the hoppers above the blast furnaces and add a second hopper feeding downward in the corner as shown.

5

Place 13 more hoppers, with 6 feeding into the chests, 6 feeding into the newly placed hoppers and 1 feeding into the corner hopper as shown.

6

Add 9 more hoppers, with 8 on the back row feeding toward the left-hand side and 1 feeding downward in the corner.

COAL GOES IN HERE

ORES GO IN HERE

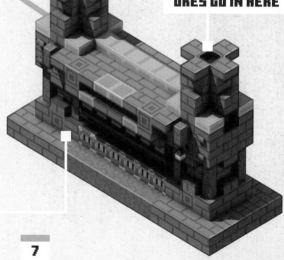

7

Finally, decorate the smelting station in your chosen theme. I included 2 chimneys, using the left side for coal and the right side for ores.

EXTRA STORAGE

Is your furnace not smelting all your ores? Add hoppers and chests below your furnaces to increase how much processed ore can be stored between visits. You can add as many hoppers and chests as you need.

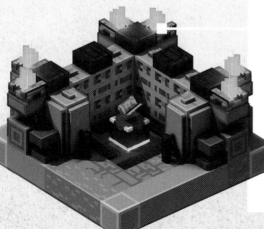

ENCHANTMENTS

There are a couple of brilliant spells that have helped me create the hoard. Meet the left and right hands of my success: fortune and efficiency. This mighty pair will earn you more than emeralds. Fortune increases the number of blocks dropped when mining and efficiency increases the speed at which you mine.

NETHERITE

If you craft your tools from netherite, they will float in lava and not get destroyed – a great way to secure your diamond tools against untimely deaths.

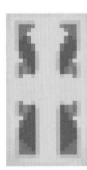

SWEET KINGDOM

Welcome to Candyland, where everything is sugary sweet, tidy and neat.
We've got peppermint treats, bouncy seats and even marshmallow streets! I've
been building a confectioner's paradise and I want YOU to be the first guest.
Everything here is edible so eat to your heart's content! Except the mushrooms.
Those are vegetables. *Yuck.*

FLAVOR FACTORY
My team of confectioners are
always busy inventing delicious
new flavors.

CHOCOLATE BRIDGE
My latest addition – a bridge
made of chocolate!

MISS LOLLY DELIGHT
Candy Queen

BOUNCY JELLY CASTLE
The doorways are extra-large so the guests don't knock their heads as they bounce from room to room.

MUSHROOM MEADOWS

SLUSHIE TAP
Thick with sugary goodness.

RAINBOW ROAD
Follow the rainbow road to Candyland.

HONEY MOAT

BUILD TECHNIQUES

My Sweet Kingdom is all set to expand. At the heart of my base is the super-factory that produces all the blocks I need to keep on building. What do you think I should add next?

BOUNCY JELLY CASTLE

This special castle design is my very own creation. Unlike any other castle ever built, this one has bouncy floors. Pretty sweet, huh?

CANDY CANE

Recognize the red and white stalks that line my buildings? Those are candy canes and I've used them as support structures throughout my base. They also look great as arches!

COTTON CANDY TREES

SLIME CARPET

I replaced the entire floor with slime blocks and carpets to create a bouncy castle. Unfortunately, drinks are no longer allowed. Someone just had to spill their slushie while bouncing!

DOUGHNUT DORMS

I've built an on-site dorm for all my factory workers – they are the ones who make the dream happen. I want them to think about sugary treats all day, every day, so I built the dorms the shape of a massive doughnut. I wonder if they can see right through my ploy.

ALPINE ARCHITECTURE

I looked to the Alps when planning my epic base. My ambitious goal was to incorporate the mountains, rivers and other natural features into my sweet empire. The setting lent itself nicely to some of the buildings I included in my base.

YUCKY MUSHROOM TAP

My base does have one tiny little secret. It is true, I haven't quite found a way to stop the mushrooms from growing. That's why when no one is watching, I pick them and flush them down the back toilet. The fungi are just too persistent! Ewww, it's so disgusting.

LOLLIPOP TOWERS

CHALETS

The small buildings in my base are chalets. These remote huts are built for mountains, with thick walls to keep the cold out and sloped roofs to stop snow from piling up high. They fit perfectly among the mountains and rivers.

USEFUL FEATURES

Every confectioner's paradise needs a few essentials. These machines give me the freedom to create as much as I like! Central to it all is my flavor factory, containing all the farms I need.

CANDY FACTORY

To get this candy factory running, I need to farm sugar, wheat, dairy and other secret ingredients. My flavor factory streamlines the process by packing in all these farms into one compact building.

CANDY CANE LIGHT

More candy canes, woohoo! This time I added lanterns so they can be lampposts.

RAINBOW ROAD

Follow the rainbow road to visit everything the Sweet Kingdom has to offer.

WHEAT FARM

I created a tiered farmland with water dispensers connected to a lever along the top to grow wheat. When the crops are ready to be harvested, I just pull the lever and then replant the seeds. I can make this farm as large or small as I like.

SUGAR CANE

Sugar cane can grow up to 4 blocks tall when planted beside water. Maximize your harvest by collecting 3 sugar canes at a time. This way you don't need to plant it again.

PIPING HOT PIPES

The factory is interconnected with a network of pipes. These pipes are not functional, but they fit perfectly with my industrial-scale flavor factory theme. I built them using gray concrete.

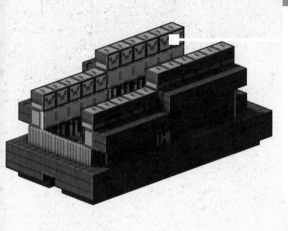

SUGAR CANE FARM

I had to mass produce this farm to meet my sugar demands. It's super simple, I planted some sugar cane and then stacked a wooden block, piston and observer atop each other. When the sugar cane grows too high, the observer activates the piston to cut it down again. See? Simple!

CUCKOO CLOCK

The cuckoo comes out of the clock at break time to call the workers out for their cookie break.

CHICKEN COOP FARM

Good quality eggs are essential to good quality baking. I collect my eggs from this luxurious chicken coop, fitted with nest perches and the softest green carpet.

THE MACABRE MOTEL

Boo! Gotcha! Look lively, my good students – you're about to enter the house of the dead. These motel grounds are littered with the undead remains of the many unfortunate adventurers who decided to stay the night and were never seen alive again. Mind your step, there are more than a few spooktacular surprises awaiting past the gates.

FORSAKEN FOREST
A tree canopy keeps the forest floor in darkness. The shade provides undead mobs with limited sanctuary during daylight hours.

DECREPIT WOOD
Crimson and warped wood are perfect for scare houses.

SOUL LIGHTING
Oooooh ... ominous. The blue lighting is powered by souls from the Nether dimension.

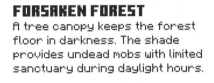

RITA THE REANIMATOR
Harbinger of Doom

PHANTOMS CIRCLING
There's no rest for the wicked. Phantoms circle around overhead, waiting for sleep-deprived adventurers.

THUNDER AND LIGHTNING
Perfect weather for a stay at the Macabre Motel.

BONE TREE
Red weeping vines hang from its branches.

HEDGE MAZE
Can you navigate through the maze? Enter at your own risk!

MOONLIT MORTUARY

BUILD TECHNIQUES

The Macabre Motel keeps guests in a permanent state of alert. There's no easy way in, out or even around the motel. My epic base is for the thrill-seekers out there!

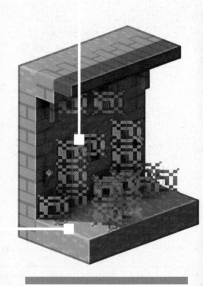

PRINCESS'S PRISON

This apartment is called the Princess's Prison, aptly named after the current inhabitant. The princess and her staff have been infected by a zombie and must remain locked up.

STICKY SITUATION

Cobwebs reduce player movement to 15% and take an astonishing 13 seconds to traverse. I simply *had* to create a defense feature with them! The perimeter of my base is lined with these sticky blocks – intruders must follow the existing paths or risk being exposed and vulnerable. Cobwebs can be obtained using shears.

TRICKY PATHS

Scatter cobwebs along the path in uneven patterns. Navigating past the cobwebs will be much harder when you can't guess where they will appear next!

SWAMPLAND

I built the motel with mossy cobblestone and vines to blend into the swamp environment.

SKELETAL STABLES

I cater to a rather niche group of tenants, so naturally some of the features of my base are a little unique. My stables, for example, are for skeleton horses only.

GRAVEYARD CRYPTS

The graveyard is the most visited spot in my base. Almost all my guests end up buried here. Graveyards are spooky and sinister – perfect for my motel. I used a mix of old, decrepit gravestones and highly extravagant crypts to give my base an aged and rustic feel.

THUNDER AND LIGHTNING

Skeleton horses are usually very rare. Luckily, the frequent thunderstorms above the motel cause many unfortunate horses to turn into skeleton horsemen. I quickly dispatch the riders and lead the skeleton horses to my stables.

SECRET PATHS

With so many traps around, I decided it was prudent to create a series of safe routes in and out of my maze. These "safe" routes are discreetly hidden and only I know how to find them.

WICKED TREES

Build custom natural-looking features to make your base unique. I constructed dead trees and fossil-like bone structures to make the base more wicked and macabre.

BLOCK CHOICE

Nether resources are perfect for a spooky theme. The dark and vivid colors seem to carry a sense of foreboding. Perfect! Add cobwebs around the base for extra spooky effect.

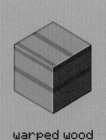

warped wood

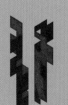

weeping vines

iron bars

bone

I've come up with some special home-made drinks and activities to keep my guests entertained. What better way to welcome an old friend than with a quick potion of bad luck followed by a race through the Macabre Maze?

CONCOCTIONS

I concoct all manner of corrupt potions for my guests. Nothing more fun than hiding around corners throwing splash potions at unsuspecting players! I like to start with a potion of bad luck to set the mood and then quickly follow up with a potion of weakness or nausea for extra fun.

SPLASH POTION

Splash potions are brewed by adding gunpowder to normal potions. Brew up some horrible potions to throw at players!

POTIONS ROOM

I keep a well-stocked lab on my base in order to have a constant supply of potions for my ghastly night games. Essential to this room is my endless water source in the center of the lab, made from water sources at both ends of a 3x1 trough.

ELYTRA LAUNCH POINT

ELYTRA ROOM

The modern witch no longer travels by broomstick. No, nowadays we travel in style with a stack of fireworks and a trusty elytra cape. Helmets are recommended.

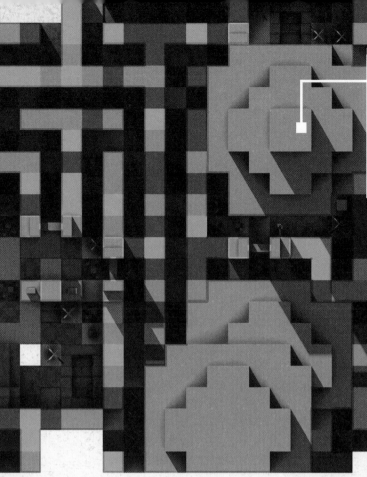

MACABRE MAZE

Thinking of spending a night of fun and games at the Macabre Motel? Come right in and immerse yourself in the Macabre Maze. With dropping floors, changing passages and hidden rooms, you're sure to have a blast! Keep your wits about you – there's more to the maze than meets the eye.

MAZE MECHANICS

The maze is littered with a series of traps and surprises to keep guests on their toes. Look out for sweet berries cutting at your ankles, trip wires unleashing arrows, dispensers pouring molten lava and iron doors leading to hazardous crypts. There's much, much more but I'll leave you to experience those on your own.

CRYPT DWELLERS

The stone doors to these crypts are time-locked with a daylight sensor. As soon as the sun goes down, their inhabitants arise.

SECRET DOOR

I've hidden secret passages throughout the motel so I can dash between rooms unseen. I make sure to hide the passages discreetly behind bookshelves and paintings, so my guests don't accidentally find them.

73

PHOENIX CASTLE

Enter, enter! My friends, ride on in and I'll show you around. This is the last true outpost against the dark forces that pillage the land. Built to repel the most persistent of invaders, Phoenix Castle has never fallen to hostile forces – nor shall it on my watch! What are you waiting for? Come on in and *do not let anything in behind you!*

SIEGE SUPPLIES
Many crops grow within the castle walls. We shall never succumb to a siege!

PARAPET
The parapet is manned day and night, lest we get caught unawares.

MOAT
Vicious guardians live in this moat.

SIR CORNELIUS LUCKLESS
Paranoid Knight

74

CASTLE
The thick stone walls of the castle are sure to keep intruders at bay.

CURTAIN WALL
Steep, unscalable walls stop the most arduous invaders.

VILLAGE

BUILD TECHNIQUES

My fellow builders may brand me the paranoid knight, but I assure you I wear this label as a badge of honor. Preparedness is no laughing matter, and I'm ready to wager *my* base will be the last one standing when the illagers breach the final frontier.

CASTLE INTERIOR

This huge castle is absolutely jam-packed with rooms of every function. There are kitchens, dorms, stables, armories – you name it, I have it!

BANNERS

Every lord needs an emblem and mine is the phoenix. It represents my motto *"RUN AWAY TO LIVE ANOTHER DAY."*

ROYAL CHAMBER

With a balcony for archers and sentry posts for men-at-arms, my royal chamber is the safest room in the castle.

CONTROL ROOM

I have many, many nasty little traps around my base. I control them all from here in my control room.

STABLES

Riders can race their horses all the way into the secure castle and to the stables. From there they must forgo their weapons and make their way on foot.

STOCKROOM

I've begun stockpiling for the inevitable siege. I don't know who will come for me – or when – but I'm no fool. I am prepared.

ESCAPE TUNNEL

TURRET

I've built this same tower four times in the creation of my castle. It's highly defensible: look closely and you can see the arrow-slit windows and trapdoor mechanisms I use to rain terror on the invaders below.

FLYING BUTTRESSES

The castle walls are lined at regular intervals by buttress bastions. There's no mistaking these fortifications as a public warning against hostile forces.

BATTERED FORTIFICATIONS

My stone walls have seen some heavy action, as is evident by the abused facade. You can mimic this style by alternating between stone, mossy cobblestone, andesite, stone bricks and stair equivalents. Make sure you don't inadvertently create a parkour staircase of jutting rocks.

FLAG

Every castle needs a flag. All who see my flags billowing in the air atop the tallest peaks of the castle will know that Sir Cornelius Luckless defends this land. Keep an eye out for foot soldiers carrying my standard forward into battle. I will be there in spirit!

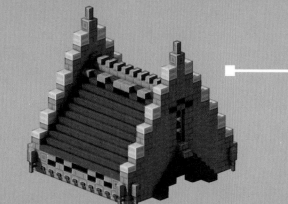

ROOF SLATING

I used traditional roof slating to top my buildings. There's nothing complicated here – just lines of wooden staircases with stone faces. Add windows for extra lighting.

USEFUL FEATURES

MOB HOUSES AND TRIPWIRES

To the unassuming eye, the townhouses around my castle look like villager dwellings. It is but a cruel trick – they are actually filled with the most horrible mobs. Tripwires are connected to the doorways and exits, ensnaring invaders who breach the perimeter.

The castle is the product of intensive research. I carefully considered every element of the base before construction. It is a true bastion against evil, jam-packed with deadly traps and cunning tricks to repel the most perseverant of hostile mobs. If not, there's always the "last resort"...

OUT WITH A BANG

TNT is, in my opinion, the best way to dispatch adversaries. Of all the mobs and traps that protect my castle, it is the TNT scatterbomb trap that gives me the most reassurance. No one will survive a blast from this explosive rig.

LAST RESORT

If I am forced to leave my castle behind, I have taken extraordinary measures to ensure my unwanted guests receive a warm welcome: the escape tunnel is lined with TNT and rigged to blow with the press of a button. Gravel is piled high in the ceiling, waiting to fall and block the passage. This is my "last resort."

GATE GUARDIANS

The first line of defense is the classic moat. Deep and filled with guardians, this excavated trench is a nuisance to all diggers and breachers alike.

BATTLEMENTS

I've lined the battlements with lava-filled dispensers. Any players foolish enough to scale my walls will find themselves in very hot water!

CONTROL PANEL

The traps around my base are connected to this panel. Just one quick flick of a lever and some unfortunate intruder will meet their fate.

CASTLE SCONCES

Sconces are the perfect torch holders for castles. Here I've used a torch, a frame and a slab. It's important to place each item in the correct order: first a torch, then a frame and finally a slab. Top tip: try replacing the slab with other blocks to see what combination you like most.

MAZE-LIKE PLANNING

The castle grounds have intentionally been laid out to be as puzzling as possible, with lots of dead ends and backtracking passages. My loyal soldiers will rain hellfire from above as the invaders figure out how to reach the castle.

CRAFTHOLME

Crowned the architectural jewel of the realm, Craftholme is HQ to the Twelve. As the largest and tallest construction yet built, Craftholme is a beacon of civilization and an intellectual lighthouse in this dark age. A citadel for adventurers and creators alike, Craftholme has all the accessories and fixtures for budding young architects ready to plan their next epic base.

OUTDOOR FORUM

PULPIT
The daily announcements are broadcast from this pulpit. Tune in to hear the latest news.

CRANES/TETHERS

ENTRYWAY
Bridges to raised entryways bottleneck intruders into a tight and vulnerable position.

BRIDGE

EXTERIOR

ESCHER WONDER
Grand Architect & Guild Leader

Craftholme is renowned as the most prestigous architecture school in the realm. At any given moment, numerous students and teachers alike can be found working on new, avant-garde bases. Many of the bases toured today were first conceived in these rooms.

GREAT BELL
The pealing of this great bell resonates through the valleys and can be heard at great distances.

CHANDELIER

GRAND LIBRARY

BLOCK MUSEUM

It is good practice for all crafters to understand the blocks they are working with. Students can come here to view and study all the blocks in Minecraft.

MOLTEN VENT

Building atop lava springs provides a great natural defense. Intruders who attempt to burrow in will have a molten cascade to contend with.

INDOOR FARM

This indoor farm was initially a research project for growing crops in the Nether. Though unsuccessful, it is still in constant use and its crops go to support the victims of Nether invasions.

FORGE

BUILD TECHNIQUES

Craftholme's beauty comes from the many details on its exterior. I picked sandstone and red sandstone as my primary blocks and built features that supported these colors.

BALCONY

Much of Craftholme's magic comes from the spectacular views. Large windows, balconies and open-air forums provide a lot of clear light and fresh air to the inhabitants. Take a look at all those views!

ENTRYWAY

A citadel, by design, must be defensible. I used an old medieval trick to build this entryway. As you can see, the doorway is only accessible via an elevated walkway, making it much harder for intruders to gain entry, while leaving them exposed to attacks from above.

FACADE

The citadel's facade walks a fine line between aesthetics and durability. Though lined with exposed windows and scaleable blocks, the walls are also tall and thick and will not be easily penetrated.

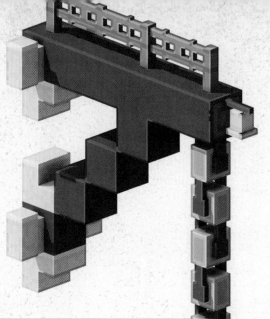

PULPIT

Raised high above the ground, towering above courtyards and balconies, the pulpit is where I address the students and townsfolk below. Whether it's to hear the daily public announcements, to celebrate seasonal festivities or to respond to a rallying call-to-arms, this is where the public goes to find out the latest information.

CRANE

Huge construction cranes line the walls. They act as tethers for airships and levers for construction. The chain effect is produced by stacking grindstones.

BLOCK CHOICES

The pulpit was an opportunity to pack some color into the build. Green awnings, yellow banners and note blocks stand out nicely against the sandstone.

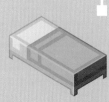
green bed

acacia slab   note block

WALL AND WINDOW DETAIL

These stylish walls are lined with lots of narrow, tall windows. They are an excellent source of natural light, and work perfectly as murder holes through which to fire projectiles at hostile players. Build these with staircases – they are easy to shoot out of but difficult to shoot into.

USEFUL FEATURES

COUNCIL TABLE
Much like the fabled Arthurian Round Table, the circular shape of the council table implies there is no head and that everyone is of equal status. It is of great symbolic significance.

The council chamber is the pride and joy of my base. I pulled out all the stops here, using every tool at my disposal to make it look the part. There's no mistaking this chamber as the heart of lawmaking in the realm.

CHAIR
The Twelve meet in this chamber to discuss matters of great importance. Each has their own great chair made from trapdoors, a stair block and a banner. That looks comfy!

THE GREAT BELL
The great bell is one of my favorite features – the citadel would be incomplete without it. Anyone can add a bell in the town center, but a great big bell like this? That's some expert level construction work!

SHUTTERS
These windows can't remain open all the time. What if it rains? No, there are too many precious items that could get damaged to risk that. If you don't want windows, you should consider trapdoors. One of their properties is to block water – that's just one of the many things we teach the students here at Craftholme.

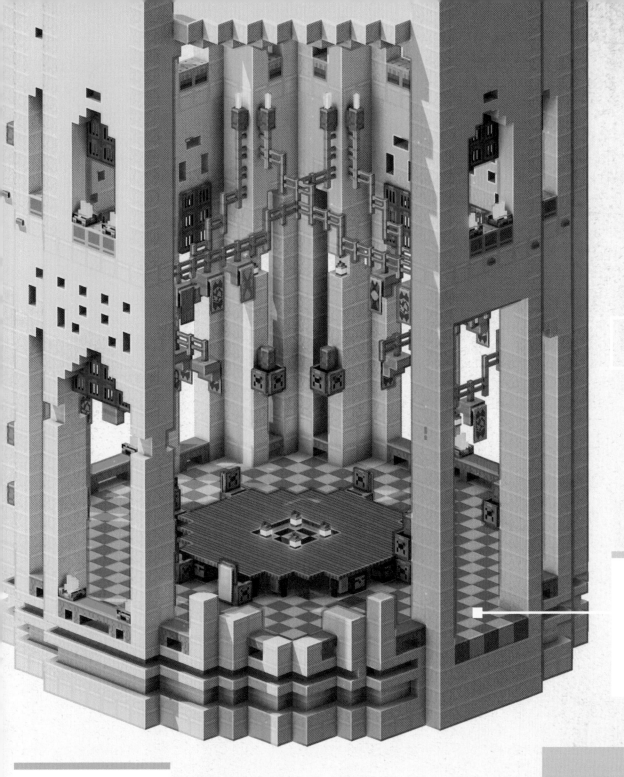

CHANDELIER

A central, old-fashioned chandelier is a novel way to fill in a cavernous room. It occupies the space while giving the chamber grandiosity. A classy light for a classy room.

COUNCIL CHAMBER

With only a large table and chairs, the council chamber serves only one purpose: good-natured debate.

BANNER HOLDER

Banners are great hanging directly on the wall but in a room where every detail is meticulously planned, I felt I had to give them a little extra. These simple trapdoor and fence bindings are compact and give the room more of a wow factor.

HANG LIGHTS

Soaring high ceilings look great but they are a lighting logistical nightmare. My lighting solutions use glowstones surrounded by a variety of trapdoors. I placed a mix of these wherever I needed more lighting and suspended them from the ceiling with fence blocks.

GOODBYE

Well, well, well, it seems we've reached the end of our tour. I have to say, I'm impressed! I thought my base was going to be the best, but honestly, I can't decide which base I like most. They are all so unique, each with their own style and special features. Did you see the cannon on *Fenrir's Tooth*? I need to get myself one of those! And a floating Nether portal? I never thought of that before. I don't know about you, but I've certainly learned a trick or two when it comes to building epic bases.

Is that a sparkle in your eye? It seems to me you've been inspired to create your own epic base. What will you build next? An underwater palace? A floating fortress? A candy kingdom?

And now it's time to say goodbye. Stay tuned for more epic builds from our ever-growing team of expert builders. Do you have what it takes to join the ranks?

THE OFFICIAL GUIDEBOOKS

GUIDE TO:
CREATIVE

GUIDE TO:
SURVIVAL

UPDATED EDITION OF GUIDE TO: EXPLORATION

GUIDE TO:
THE NETHER & THE END

GUIDE TO:
REDSTONE

GUIDE TO:
ENCHANTMENTS & POTIONS

GUIDE TO:
FARMING

GUIDE TO:
PVP MINIGAMES

GUIDE TO:
OCEAN SURVIVAL

GUIDE TO
MINECRAFT DUNGEONS

A HANDBOOK FOR HEROES

Learn about the latest Minecraft guidebooks
at **ReadMinecraft.com**

DEL REY

MOJANG